CONTENTS

T0349765

INTRODUCTION

Mushrooms are one of the most ubiquitous, yet also most mysterious, life forms on planet Earth. They are neither plants nor animals, but, as members of the fungi kingdom, share characteristics with both of those groups. They can contain enough poison to kill a human, or enough medicinal compounds to help fight cancer and dementia. Other mushrooms have hallucinogenic qualities that can alter our perceptions and transform our experience of the world.

Over thousands of years and across continents, mushrooms have held many meanings for people of different cultures. They've been perceived as tools to aid spiritual journeys, gifts from the gods, and wellsprings of healing and longevity; the inspiration behind all types of art, sources of folk stories and superstitions; and the basis of many nutritious, delicious meals.

With modern scientific and ecological research, mushrooms have come to mean even more to us humans. We've begun to understand how fungi hold together entire ecosystems, and we've looked to mushrooms to help clean up environmental disasters. We've explored how mushrooms can protect our immune systems and treat diseases like HIV and

THE LITTLE BOOK OF
MUSHROOMS

FELICITY HART

summersdale

THE LITTLE BOOK OF MUSHROOMS

Text by Stephanie Parent

An Hachette UK Company
www.hachette.co.uk

Summersdale Publishers Ltd
Part of Octopus Publishing Group Limited
Carmelite House
50 Victoria Embankment
LONDON
EC4Y 0DZ
UK

www.summersdale.com

Printed and bound in Poland

ISBN: 978-1-80007-387-6

Substantial discounts on bulk quantities of Summersdale books are available to corporations, professional associations and other organizations. For details contact general enquiries: telephone: +44 (0) 1243 771107 or email: enquiries@summersdale.com.

Disclaimer
Neither the author nor the publisher can be held responsible for any loss, damage or injury – be it health, financial or otherwise – arising out of the use, or misuse, of the suggestions made herein. It's always advisable to consult a physician before making any changes to your diet.

depression. We've even identified fungi as a key to creating human habitats on other planets.

In this book, we'll survey the historical legacies and modern possibilities of mushrooms, as well as the fascinating variety within the mushroom kingdom. We'll look at ancient cave art depicting fungi, mushrooms on the moon and Mars, and everything in between. We'll also explore many common mushroom species you can search for in a woodland or park near you, or even in your own backyard. And in the final chapter, you'll find delicious recipes, so you can sample the culinary possibilities mushrooms have to offer.

Once you've read about the many forms that mushrooms can take, and the amazing fungi facts scientists continue to uncover, you'll never think of a mushroom as just a simple cap and stem again.

CHAPTER 1

MEET THE MUSHROOM

Most of us think of mushrooms as a delicious part of a risotto or soup, or as an interesting feature we notice on a walk through the woods. Yet we may not consider just how different mushrooms are from the other vegetable ingredients in our salad, or the flora we encounter on a hike. This chapter explores the mushroom's unique makeup as part of the fungi kingdom and examines how mushrooms interact with and support other life forms on Earth — including humans.

WHAT IS A MUSHROOM?

While many of us group mushrooms among the flora we see in the wild, or the plants we forage or cultivate for food, mushrooms actually aren't part of the plant kingdom at all. Rather, mushrooms, along with yeasts and moulds, belong to a unique group of organisms called fungi. A few key differences separate fungi from other biological "kingdoms", such as plants, animals and bacteria. For instance, fungi digest their food *outside* of their bodies — a process we'll explore in depth later in this chapter.

Fungi are also distinguished by the composition of their cells: mushroom cell walls are made of chitin, a cellulose-like material formed from sugar molecules. You will recognize chitin as the same substance that makes up the exoskeletons of crustaceans like crabs and lobsters, and insects such as spiders and beetles.

Finally, fungi differ from other organisms in the way they grow. Most fungi create spores: seed-like particles that disperse into the air and thus facilitate reproduction. Mushrooms grow visible spore-producing structures called sporocarps, or fruit bodies — these structures are the part of a mushroom we see and sometimes consume.

THE MARVEL OF MUSHROOM GROWTH

When we think of mushrooms, we picture the visible fruit bodies described on the previous page — but the life of a mushroom begins with processes human eyes rarely see. Just as plants grow from seeds buried in the soil, mushrooms develop from microscopic fungal spores that have found a dark, humid place full of decaying plant matter — i.e. fungi food.

Moisture allows mushroom spores to germinate and grow thin, tubular threads called hyphae. The tips of the hyphae release digestive enzymes into decomposing organic matter, such as tree roots, bark or fallen leaves. These enzymes then break down starches within the plant matter, forming simple glucose molecules that the hyphae can absorb through their tips. Thus, digestion occurs *outside* of the fungi!

Once the hyphae take in nutrients, they continue to grow longer, eventually forming an interconnected mass of hyphae threads called a mycelium. Mycelium grows from the tips of the hyphae, spreading upward and outward like vines, seeking even more organic matter to break down and absorb.

WHERE DO MUSHROOMS GROW?

Now that you understand the mycelial network, you might guess — correctly — that many mushrooms grow in the woods. Mushrooms often form at the base of trees, where they take nourishment from decaying tree bark and roots. Because mushroom spores and hyphae need ample moisture, they populate humid spaces. Mushrooms do not obtain food from the sun as plants do, so they tend to grow in shady spots.

Some mushrooms feed off of faecal matter, and thus pop up near deposits of animal dung. Other fungi consume wood and can grow high up on tree trunks; others eat almost completely decomposed plants in gardens or compost piles.

While the mycelial network thrives all year long, ideal weather conditions — namely prolonged humidity or rain — cause mushrooms to produce visible fruit bodies that release spores. Air currents carry these tiny spores to new areas where, if the spores find decaying matter to feed on, more mushrooms will grow.

Mushrooms, and fungi in general, are an incredibly widespread group of organisms that exist on every continent in the world. Mushrooms have even been found underwater and growing from moss in Antarctica.

✳ THE MIGHTY MYCELIAL NETWORK ✳

As the mycelium grows upward and outward, it multiplies so much that it can be thought of as an entire network of fungi — a web that is incredibly dense. One network of interconnected mycelium, if laid flat, could extend thousands of kilometres.

Not only does this mycelial network produce mushroom fruit bodies, but it also ensures the health of the plant life around it. As the hyphae break down nutrients to aid their own growth, these nutrients — including nitrogen, phosphorus, magnesium and other minerals — become easier for surrounding plants to absorb.

Because of mycelium's web-like nature, it can cover a great surface area, and the tiny hyphae within mycelium can manoeuvre around rocks and other obstacles that impede tree roots. The mycelial network thus reaches further into the environment than plants themselves can, and it brings all the nourishment it finds back to the trees.

The mycelial network doesn't just support the tree where the fungi first developed; as this network spreads across forests, it connects multiple trees of different species. Incredibly, trees can actually communicate with each other by transmitting chemical signals along the mycelial network, with trees that need more nutrients calling for help from older, larger trees. "Hub" or "mother" trees, with their deeper roots and greater access to water, sunlight and nutrients, then send minerals and sugars along the mycelial network to the saplings in need of support.

In addition to communicating a need for nutrition or transporting nutrients themselves, trees can also warn of potential danger along the fungi network. For example, when invasive species attack, trees send a "heads-up" to nearby plants. A University of Manchester study found that when trees were overrun by aphids, nearby trees that had not yet encountered the aphids, but that were linked to the damaged trees by a mycelial network, also produced chemicals to repel aphids.

The transfer of information and resources through the mycelial network is so complex that researchers have compared it to the internet, calling it the "wood-wide web".

THE MULTITASKING MUSHROOM

We've seen the geographical breadth of mushroom growth, and we've looked at how the mycelial network can connect entire forests even when mushroom fruit bodies aren't visible. But mushrooms have many other impressive features and functions in the natural world. For instance, as mycelium breaks down and consumes organic matter, it can also remove harmful substances from earth and water. The mycelium eats bacteria that would otherwise sicken plants.

Mushrooms also provide a natural recycling system: they literally "eat up" the dead leaves and branches that would otherwise linger as debris on the forest floor, and then return the nutrients from these dead plant parts to the soil. Some fungi consume, and thus dispose of, dead animal bodies as well.

In addition to cleaning up dead plant and animal matter, mushrooms also offer benefits to living animals in the woods. Mushroom fruit bodies provide food for insect larvae, snails and small mammals, and as fungi cause tree trunks and fallen logs to decompose further, they create spaces for birds, mice and squirrels to nest.

THE MUSHROOM–HUMAN CONNECTION

The relationship between humans and mushrooms extends not only through all of human history, but even further into the past. Believe it or not, mushrooms are closer relatives to human beings than to plants!

Around 1.1 billion years ago, a single-celled organism that contained characteristics of both animals (a sperm-like feature) and fungi (stronger, cellulose-like cell walls) branched away from the plant kingdom. This rudimentary organism continued to develop into many more complex creatures, including animals, humans and fungi. As a result of this common ancestor, humans share more DNA with mushrooms than mushrooms do with plants. The proteins within fungi appear more similar to animal than plant proteins as well.

Not only are humans and fungi biologically related, but humans have eaten mushrooms as far back as the Stone Age — mushroom spores were found in the teeth of a prehistoric woman buried almost 19,000 years ago. Records show that mushrooms were consumed in ancient Aztec, Roman, Greek and Egyptian civilizations.

In addition to consuming mushrooms, humans have relied on fungi for medicinal purposes for thousands of years, all over the world. Indigenous tribes of North America made powders from puffball mushrooms to stop bleeding and heal wounds. In ancient Chinese medicine, reishi mushrooms were taken to prevent illness. A 4,000-year-old corpse in what is now the Austrian-Italian border was found carrying a birch polypore mushroom, which has antibiotic and antiparasitic qualities.

In modern times, scientists have continued to research and apply the medical benefits of mushrooms, and they've determined that the same chemicals that protect fungi in the wild also benefit the human immune system. It's yet another human-mushroom link that promises further innovation, as we continue to learn more about mushrooms and how they could help us treat cancer, improve brain health and much more.

In addition to accessing mushrooms' healing powers, humans have used mushrooms — particularly Psilocybe mushrooms with hallucinogenic properties — as part of spiritual and religious traditions throughout history. Archaeologists have discovered images of Psilocybe mushrooms in prehistoric cave art of Europe and Africa, and the Mayans used mushrooms in religious rituals as long ago as 1,000 BCE.

THE MUSHROOM'S MANY IDENTITIES

Overall, about 14,000 distinct species of mushrooms have been identified — and scientists believe we've only discovered a small portion of the fungal variety in the world. Some of these mushrooms are edible and highly nutritious, while others are poisonous to humans; some provide medical benefits, while others produce an altered mental state when ingested. Some have fantastical appearances: morels look like a honeycomb or sponge, and enokitake grow in groups of long, thin stalks that resemble a clump of straw.

When it comes to understanding just how crucial mushrooms are to life on Earth, and what benefits they can provide to humankind, we've only uncovered the tip of the iceberg. Or, in a more apt metaphor, we've just seen the surface of the vast mycelium.

We'll explore many amazing varieties, features and uses of mushrooms in greater detail throughout this book. But first, in the next chapter, let's look at the fascinating anatomy of the mushroom fruit body itself.

CHAPTER 2

MUSHROOM ANATOMY

As we've learned, the mushroom fruit bodies — or sporocarps — we forage, eat and use as medicine are only the visible part of a much larger mycelial network. This underground web of hyphae threads, which can persist and expand for thousands of years, forms the backbone of mushroom anatomy. The days-to-weeks-long life of a sporocarp might seem ephemeral, even insignificant in comparison. However, within its short life span, a fruiting body enables fungi to protect itself and reproduce. In this chapter, we'll take a close look at what makes a fruiting body, and how this relates to its function.

THE MUSHROOM FRUIT BODY

With the widely varying species of mushrooms identified so far, it would be impossible to create one definitive image of mushroom anatomy. After all, some mushrooms are shaped like the human ear, others like a lacy veil or a turkey's tail!

For our overview, we'll focus first on the anatomy of basidiomycetes — the fungi we most likely think of when we picture mushrooms. While basidiomycetes are technically distinguished by their club-shaped reproductive organs, known as basidia, we can also characterize this group as including the typical toadstool-type mushroom, with its rounded cap and stem rising from the earth.

As we'll learn, this mushroom's shape helps it to protect and release reproductive particles, and, ultimately, create more mushrooms. Turn the page to learn more about their anatomy.

THE MUSHROOM'S ESSENTIAL PARTS

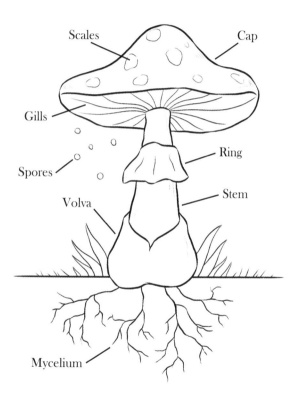

Scales

Cap

Gills

Spores

Ring

Volva

Stem

Mycelium

THE UNIVERSAL VEIL

When a mushroom first emerges from the earth, a universal veil that resembles an eggshell often shelters the immature fruit body from the elements. This membrane-like veil eventually breaks open and allows the sporocarp to emerge — but veil remnants linger as part of the mature mushroom's anatomy.

The bottom of the universal veil sometimes becomes a cup-shaped volva at the base of the mushroom. The volva might be partly or totally buried beneath the earth, but it's worth looking out for: many mushrooms with volvas are part of the Amanita species and are poisonous to humans.

While volvas appear at the base of a mushroom, veil remnants also sit atop the mushroom in the form of scales. These scales form a hard plate that protects the mushroom cap, just as the entire veil once did.

Finally, parts of the veil sometimes persist around the stems of mature mushrooms, forming circles known as rings. The material, shape and positioning of a mushroom's ring are useful tools to help identify its species.

✳ CAP, GILLS AND SPORES: THE ✳ MUSHROOM'S ALL-IMPORTANT CROWN

Once the universal veil breaks, the mushroom's reproductive elements — the cap, gills and spores — are exposed. The cap, or pileus, is exactly what it sounds like: a covering that protects spore-producing surfaces, the same way a hat shields us from rain. The pileus can be flat or rounded and comes in many colours and textures, from smooth to bumpy, scaly to pitted. Like the rings and volva, a cap's particular characteristics provide clues to the mushroom's species.

The cap's most important role is to shelter the spore-producing gills, or lamellae, that hang from its underside. Lamellae usually consist of thin, papery layers that resemble a fish's gills, but some mushrooms have differently shaped structures. Bracket or shelf fungi have spore-producing pores on their underside; these mushrooms protrude from tree trunks like shelves. The aptly named lion's mane and bearded tooth mushrooms feature spore-producing substances that resemble teeth or strands of hair.

Because mushroom gills are highly compressed, they allow for a large surface area relative to the mushroom's mass — and more surface area means more spores can be produced and dispersed.

Whatever shape the lamellae take, if a mushroom is among the basidiomycetes we've discussed so far, the gills will contain reproductive structures called basidia. These microscopic spore-producing organs take the shape of clubs or pedestals that support the spores on their surfaces.

Spores themselves are one-celled organisms so small that 25,000 of them would only cover one pinhead. Yet these tiny organisms are mighty — just as a seed germinates into a plant, each spore can grow enough hyphae to create a new fungus.

Some spores leave the mushroom actively, through a phenomenon known as Buller's drop: a water-and-sugar droplet that, thanks to the humidity between gills, accumulates on the edge of each basidium. Condensation also gathers atop the spores themselves, and eventually these two liquids meet. As Buller's drop transfers onto the spore, the momentum and additional mass launch the spore into the air.

In other cases, spores rest passively on the gills until wind, water or the actions of animals or insects shake them loose.

THE SIMPLE BUT ESSENTIAL STEM

The stem, stalk or stipe of a mushroom is one of its most straightforward parts — it's the pole-like structure that holds up the mushroom cap and raises it above the earth. Basic as the stem may be, it is crucial to the mushroom's ability to reproduce. The stipe lifts mushroom gills higher into the air, where, once spores are actively or passively released, wind currents grab hold of these particles and carry them off, sometimes for incredible distances. One study found that high-altitude winds could transport fungal spores up to 13,500 kilometres in a week! By contrast, without a stalk, most mushrooms could only release spores within the few metres surrounding the fruit body.

Another important feature of the mushroom stem is its ability to absorb large amounts of water, thus helping the mushroom to grow taller, faster.

Although many people only eat mushroom caps, the stem holds larger amounts of minerals including iron, copper and zinc. In fact, the entire fruiting body contains the nutrients and medicinal compounds we can use — or, in other species, the poisonous toxins we need to avoid.

MUSHROOMS OF A DIFFERENT SHAPE

So far, we've looked at the anatomy of basidiomycetes: mushrooms with a cap, spore-producing gills or pores, and a stem. Now let's look at another major group, the ascomycetes. Although ascomycetes may not be what we first picture as mushrooms, they actually make up the largest category of fungi, and include mushrooms prized in gourmet cuisine — morels and truffles.

In contrast to the round-capped basidiomycetes, ascomycetes often have cup- or flask-shaped fruiting bodies. What technically differentiates these mushroom categories, however, are their reproductive mechanisms. Basidiomycetes produce spores externally, on the tips of the club-like basidia, while ascomycetes make spores internally, within sacs called asci.

The *Aleuria* mushroom pictured below, with its fluted cup shape, is an example of an ascomycete.

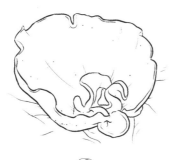

Because ascomycetes produce spores internally, inside of the microscopic asci sacs, they do not need the protective covering of a cap or the layered environment of gills. Rather, in cup-shaped ascomycetes, the asci make up most of the top surface of the cups themselves.

In other ascomycetes, the spore sacs are contained within flask-like spheres only a few millimetres wide. These tiny flasks can combine to form larger, unusual structures, as in the case of dead man's fingers — a mushroom that resembles decaying fingers rising from the earth. Another flask fungi, coal fungus, looks like a lump of black coal.

Unlike basidiomycetes, all ascomycetes release their spores actively rather than passively. The asci sacs collect water within the fruiting body's humid environment, just as the basidia in basidiomycetes do. Inside the asci, water pressure builds until the spores eject out of a pore at one end. These asci sacs thus behave like a "fungal cannon", shooting spores into the environment, where they can spread and create new mushrooms.

THE MANY USES OF THE MUSHROOM'S FRUIT BODY

Whether it resembles a toadstool's cap, a fluted vase or a clump of dead fingers, the anatomy of a mushroom fruit body is an architectural marvel that protects the growing mushroom, then produces and disperses spores, all within a few weeks. The primary purpose of the sporocarp is, of course, to ensure the fungi's continued existence and growth. However, these fruiting bodies also provide benefits to hungry animals and humans that the underground mycelium does not.

Mushroom fruit bodies are a rich source of fibre, vitamins and minerals. Sporocarps can also contain powerful active ingredients, such as health-protecting antioxidants, not found in the mycelium.

We'll explore some of these powerful ingredients, along with many other fascinating mushroom superpowers, in the next chapter.

CHAPTER 3

AMAZING MUSHROOM DISCOVERIES

Fungi are a unique and incredibly varied group of organisms, with many remarkable qualities we're just beginning to explore. Mushrooms can help us improve the health of both the natural world we all live in, and our own bodies. Fungi might even enable us to create new homes in outer space!

So many fascinating, useful, and in some cases, downright bizarre mushrooms exist that it would be impossible to cover them all in this book. In fact, we haven't even discovered them all yet. In the chapter to come, you'll learn more about both the wide-ranging benefits fungi can bring us, and some of the most memorable mushroom curiosities.

MUSHROOMS: NATURE'S SUPERHERO

In Chapter One, we looked at mushrooms' essential role in supporting the forest ecosystem, enabling trees to communicate and help each other thrive. Without mushrooms, nature would have a much harder time surviving — but fungi can go further to help humans repair some of the environmental damage we ourselves have created.

Mushrooms naturally eat up decaying plant and animal matter, thus cleaning the forest of debris. Yet fungi can also consume human-made waste, such as plastics, fossil fuels and oils, and harmful chemicals.

For example, the enzymes in oyster mushrooms break apart the hydrocarbons of petroleum and soak up poisonous heavy metals like mercury. We've used these fan-shaped fungi to help clean petroleum from Chevron oil wells in the Ecuadorian Amazon rainforest, and from the COSCO-Busan oil spill in the San Francisco Bay.

After the Sonoma County, California, wildfires of 2017, a group known as the Fire Remediation Action Coalition placed tubing containing oyster mushrooms in fire-damaged areas. The mushrooms thus absorbed toxic ash before it could infiltrate waterways and crops.

Research suggests fungi can also eat up toxic chemicals deployed in warfare, as well as pesticides. Scientists have even observed fungi naturally absorbing radiation at nuclear disaster sites like Chernobyl. However, these promising methods of chemical clean-up require more research before we put them to active use.

Mushrooms also offer a solution to the problem of plastic disposal. Non-biodegradable plastics fill landfills and oceans, but in 2011, science students discovered an Ecuadorian fungus that consumes polyurethane plastic even in airless spaces like the bottom of a landfill. Similarly, in 2017, scientists studying landfills in Pakistan realized that the mushroom *Aspergillus tubingensis* digests polyester polyurethane — the long-lasting plastic found in packing peanuts — in just a few weeks. A 2014 study used oyster and split gill mushrooms to break down plastic into an organic substance that's even safe enough for humans to ingest!

Scientists are still working on developing the technology to use fungi for plastic removal on a large scale. If research continues, we might one day eat up our old plastic in the form of a protein-rich food, created with help from the mighty mushroom.

While we don't yet use mushrooms to decompose plastic on a large scale, humans already rely on fungi to produce environmentally safe alternatives to plastic and similar materials. Companies such as Evocative Design use fungi mycelium as "glue", bonding wood shavings, hemp and other agricultural and forestry by-products to create biodegradable plastic substitutes. These include packaging that, unlike the Styrofoam filling landfills, is compostable while still protecting items during shipping. Already, major companies including IKEA and Dell have adopted mycelium-based packaging.

Mycelium-based building material can also replace concrete — a huge boon for the environment, as concrete production causes 8 per cent of CO_2 emissions worldwide. And because fungi-based materials are made with waste from the agricultural and forestry industries, they actively *reduce* environmental debris rather than adding to it.

Companies like Bolt Threads have developed mycelium-based alternatives to leather, without the environmentally damaging effects of factory farming and leather-making chemicals. Lots of brands — including US-based start-up, MyEats — use mycelium to make meat replacements, which is another way to avoid the ecological cost of factory farming.

✳ FROM EARTH'S ENVIRONMENT ✳
TO THE MOON AND MARS

Fungi have another amazing application beyond making greener packaging: they may help us explore and eventually make new homes in outer space.

One space-related innovation comes from the same radiation-eating fungi observed at nuclear disaster sites. *Cryptococcus neoformans* and *Cladosporium sphaerospermum*, fungi found at Chernobyl after the nuclear explosion, include high amounts of radiation-absorbing melanin. Scientists believe this same melanin might protect astronauts from space radiation, and are currently testing the efficacy of melanin extracted from Chernobyl's fungi at the International Space Station. One study determined that a two-millimetre-thick layer of the *Cladosporium* fungus absorbed 2 per cent of space radiation, and a 21-centimetre layer would be sufficient to protect humans. As this would obviously not be practical, scientists hope to use their finding to develop fungi-based skin creams — i.e. "space sunscreen" — or incorporate fungi into the linings of spacesuits.

People could potentially grow protective mushrooms themselves on Mars — but because the outer-space atmosphere is so cold, they would need to do so in enclosed buildings. And, incredibly, that's another problem mushrooms might solve.

Fungi may also hold the key to forming human habitats on the moon and Mars. NASA researchers in Silicon Valley have identified mycelium from a variety of fungi, including oyster and reishi mushrooms, as a potential solution to a big challenge: a need to carry all the materials to build structures from Earth into space, which would involve tremendous energy costs.

NASA scientists are working to develop a light, compact framework that contains dormant fungi hardy enough to survive the months-long trip to Mars. This skeleton structure would be unfolded on Mars or the moon and, with the help of water, the fungi would grow into a viable shelter for humans. Outer layers created from ice and bacteria would eventually kill the fungi but leave the structure intact, while making certain no mycelium grows outside the habitat, where it might compromise Mars's own environment.

On top of forming shelters, mycelium might perform other functions in space, including filtering water, creating bioluminescent lighting, and even allowing habitats to repair themselves through mycelial growth.

Another amazing potential of fungi in space would be to create soil and grow crops. While hydroponics (growing plants in water rather than soil) can cultivate plant food for small, short-term space missions, a larger space colony would need far too many supplies and machinery from Earth to make hydroponics a viable solution. To grow enough food for an entire settlement, colonizers will need soil.

Once again, fungi's remarkable abilities could come to the rescue: the same mycelium that proves so powerful on Earth, with its tiny hyphae that manoeuvre through cracks in rock, can also penetrate asteroid matter in space. NASA scientists thus plan to use fungi to break down asteroid material, filter out toxins and ultimately turn this material into fertile soil.

Space innovations involving mushrooms are still in their beginning stages; however, these same ideas can also be applied right here on Earth. As we have seen, companies are already using mycelium in building materials. Now researchers in Brazil are studying the bioluminescent qualities of certain mushrooms, which could provide environmentally sustainable lighting on Earth as well as in space.

ASTONISHING MUSHROOM ABILITIES

BIOLUMINESCENCE

Mushrooms such as the tiny *Panellus pusillus*, which resemble fairy lights, create light through a chemical reaction of the enzyme luciferin and molecular oxygen. Scientists theorize that mushrooms glow to draw insects who will disperse their spores.

BLEEDING MUSHROOMS

The white surface of the bleeding tooth fungus appears to be spotted with blood — but the mushroom is simply excreting excess water it has absorbed from the surrounding soil. A pigment within the mushroom stains this fluid bright red. Similarly, the bleeding fairy helmet mushroom emits a red latex liquid when broken or cut.

MUSHROOM INK

At the end of their life cycle, shaggy mane and ink cap mushrooms decay and transform into a black liquid. This liquid is full of spores, and its true purpose is to allow the mushroom to reproduce. However, it has actually been used as ink, and provided inspiration for the great English poet Percy Shelley.

MIRACULOUS MEDICAL MUSHROOMS

Humans have been aware of mushrooms' healing properties for millennia. In our modern era of longer lifespans and new viruses, mushrooms offer solutions to some of our greatest medical challenges.

A WEAPON AGAINST DISEASE

In 2013, Siberian researchers discovered that chaga mushroom, a centuries-old Russian folk remedy, contains antiviral activity capable of treating HIV. Chaga's betulinic acid kills cancer cells as well. As recently as 2021, scientists identified five more mushroom strains with anti-HIV properties in Thailand.

Another Thai mushroom long used in folk medicine, the horseshoe mushroom, has been found to inhibit cervical cancer cells. The Asian medicinal mushroom cordyceps has demonstrated antitumour properties, while turkey's tail can treat several cancers.

All these mushrooms contain compounds that boost immune system activity and the number of immune cells — a potent weapon against viruses and cancers. What's more, mushroom-based medicine won't attack the body's healthy cells the way, for example, other cancer treatments do, thus avoiding harmful side effects.

MUSHROOMS OF THE MIND

Mushrooms are not only useful in combatting viruses and cancers, but can also help with ailments that affect the brain and nervous system. A six-year study from Singapore determined that when people aged over 60 ate at least 300 grams of mushrooms a week, their chance of suffering mild cognitive impairment was reduced by half. Study participants ate common oyster, shiitake and button mushrooms; what links these species is ergothioneine, an antioxidant, anti-inflammatory, brain-protecting amino acid generated only by fungi and a few microbes. In addition to ergothioneine, chemicals in mushrooms like lion's mane encourage nerve regeneration, boosting the efficacy of the central nervous system.

Other fungi compounds inhibit substances that damage brain cells. A preliminary study by the Alzheimer's Drug Discovery Foundation suggested that lion's mane can go beyond preventing cognitive decline, and may help treat advanced Alzheimer's. In Japan, the Improved Dementia Association fights dementia with reishi mushrooms, which increase blood flow to the brain.

The same mushroom qualities that reduce cognitive impairment can treat other neurodegenerative diseases such as Parkinson's — but Parkinson's disease in particular may benefit from a different mushroom compound: the psychedelic known as psilocybin.

FROM PSYCHEDELIC TO ANTIDEPRESSANT – AND MORE

Humans have used psilocybin – a hallucinogenic compound found in mushrooms of the Psilocybe genus – for as many millennia as they have healing mushrooms. Yet only in the past few decades have scientists explored the medical benefits of mind-altering mushrooms.

Recent studies at Stanford and Imperial College London determined that psilocybin binds with serotonin receptors in the brain to improve mood and enables parts of the brain to connect in ways they normally don't. With large doses, such brain activity and interconnection can lead to hallucinations; but smaller doses merely allow a patient to tolerate a wider-than-normal range of emotional experience, including painful feelings – and as such the compounds show promise for treating depression and anxiety.

Johns Hopkins University researchers have zeroed in on psilocybin's potential to combat the chronic pain, depression and cognitive dysfunction associated with Parkinson's disease and multiple sclerosis. With more research, scientists hope to isolate the chemicals within Psilocybe fungi that improve emotional and cognitive regulation, while eliminating the ones that cause hallucinations. In the future, their work could lead to effective new psychiatric treatments.

WILD AND WACKY MUSHROOM TRIVIA

Fossils of gigantic mushrooms, dating back 350 to 420 million years ago, have been recorded to be up to 7.3 metres tall and almost 1 metre wide. At this time trees grew only a few metres, making these mushrooms the dominant plant forms of the era.

Certain mushrooms number among the most expensive foods worldwide: rare Japanese matsutake mushrooms sell for about US$2,000 per kilogram, while white truffles found only in Italy can cost US$20,000 per kilogram.

Some mushroom species infest the brains of insects who ingest them. Chemicals in the mushrooms compel insects to fly higher, where they'll be eaten by birds who spread fungal spores to new areas via their droppings. Other mushrooms infect ants, giving them the urge to climb plant stems, then causing a capsule of mushroom spores to literally grow out of the dying insect's body.

AMAZING ADAPTOGENS

As we've seen, mushrooms show incredible promise for treating serious physical and mental illnesses; however, fungi can also improve our everyday health and well-being. Many of the mushrooms we've identified as cancer or antiviral treatments are also adaptogens: when ingested by humans, they correct imbalances in our hypothalamic-pituitary-adrenal axis, the system that connects our nervous and hormonal systems.

Adaptogenic herbs, plants and mushrooms are so powerful because they work to maintain equilibrium, which can differ based on an individual body's needs. Research shows adaptogens support a specific protein that fights the effects of physical and mental stress, while also bolstering the body's systems so they become more resilient. The same adaptogen might stimulate a sluggish immune or nervous system, or calm an overactive one.

The chemicals within adaptogenic mushrooms likely developed to protect fungi in harsh growing conditions. Now humans can reap those same benefits through mushroom tinctures, teas and powders. Read on for some key examples.

- **Cordyceps** – Promotes physical energy and endurance. Studies on rodents and humans suggest cordyceps reduces stress caused by physically strenuous activity, such as swimming and high-altitude training.
- **Lion's mane** – Improves mental focus and memory, and may even reverse damage to the brain caused by stress. As animal studies have demonstrated, lion's mane encourages growth of brain-derived neurotrophic factor, an important element of brain health.
- **Reishi** – Studies have identified polysaccharide compounds in reishi that reduce oxidative stress, a key cause of aging, including visible skin aging. Also boosts the immune system and encourages restorative sleep.
- **Chaga** – Reduces inflammation internally and in the skin. Several studies show that chaga can decrease blood sugar levels by as much as 31 per cent, while another study demonstrates that chaga reduces harmful low-density lipoprotein (LDL) cholesterol.
- **Shiitake** – Contains polysaccharides that strengthen the immune system, and prevents immune dysfunction caused by aging. Another of shiitake's compounds, eritadenine, lowers cholesterol levels.

MUSHROOM HALL OF FAME

Largest – A honey fungus located in Oregon spans 5.6 kilometres — the surface area of 1,665 football fields — making it the world's largest fungi. Scientists estimate this mycelial marvel has existed for at least 2,400 years.

Smallest – The world's smallest mushrooms include the tiny earthstar, with its 1–3-centimetre-wide fruiting body, and the frosty bonnet, with its shiny cap ranging from 2.5 to 7.5 millimetres wide.

Most Poisonous – *Amanita phalloides*, the death cap, reigns as Earth's deadliest mushroom. Just half a cap contains enough toxins to kill an adult human, and its poison causes complete liver and kidney failure.

Most Unexpected Flavour – The bearded tooth mushroom, distinguished by its teeth-like ridges, tastes like lobster cooked in butter. Meanwhile the chicken of the woods mushroom takes its name from its chicken-like taste.

Rarest – The devil's cigar has been discovered only in central Texas and a few secluded spots in Japan. These fungi grow in a cigar-like cylinder that splits open into a star shape. Another rarity is the caterpillar fungus, which is found only in the Himalayas. This germinates inside a moth larva, kills the insect and grows out of its corpse!

Most Colourful – Many vibrant mushrooms hold keys to their appearance in their common names: the amethyst deceiver is a brilliant purple. The scarlet cup is lined with a bright red colour that shifts to orange as the fungi develops, and New Zealand's werewere-kokako mushroom is the same electric blue as the wattle of the country's kokako bird.

Another colourful mushroom is the red-and-white spotted fly agaric, which will play a starring role in our next chapter — which is about mushrooms in cultures around the world.

CHAPTER 4

MYSTERIOUS MUSHROOMS

As we've learned, humans have been aware of mushroom's medicinal and mind-altering qualities since prehistoric times. This ancient knowledge — along with the many unique, almost magical forms mushrooms can take — has led to mushrooms becoming a key part of many cultural traditions, stories and beliefs. In this chapter, we'll look at the role of fungi in cultures throughout the world, in areas from art to food, medicine to religious rituals. It's a legacy that begins before recorded history and carries us all the way to the present day.

MAGIC MUSHROOMS ACROSS THE WORLD

For most of human history, people were more interested in so-called "magic mushrooms" for their ability to induce out-of-body, out-of-this-world experiences. In this section, we'll explore how hallucinogenic mushrooms have influenced spiritual practices, folk art and beliefs across cultures and throughout history. First, though, we need to understand the qualities of two main categories of psychedelic fungi: Psilocybe mushrooms and the fly agaric species.

Psilocybe mushroom —

✳ PSYCHEDELIC MUSHROOMS ✳

PSILOCYBE MUSHROOMS

Psilocybe mushrooms grow all over the world, with the greatest variety found in Central and South America. Visually, these species don't appear particularly special: small and brown, they have a typical cap and gill structure. What sets these mushrooms apart is their chemical compound psilocybin, which, when ingested, binds with serotonin receptors in the brain to affect mood, thought and perception. Psilocybin also prevents the brain from filtering out unnecessary sensory input — thus causing an overload of sensations.

Large doses of psilocybin can bring on euphoria — or, its opposite, fear and panic. Ingesting Psilocybe mushrooms causes visual and auditory hallucinations — distortions in colours, patterns, motions or shapes of objects, and volumes or tones of sounds.

Psilocybin can make time seem to pass very slowly, giving an added significance to every moment. It can cause a sensation of being outside one's body, increase receptiveness to new ideas and foster a feeling of connection to a larger group or to nature itself. All these elements combine to create what can feel like a mystical experience, a "trip" to a different state of being — something humans have long used to aid spiritual practices and the source of the term "magic mushrooms".

FLY AGARIC

In contrast to Psilocybe mushrooms, the *Amanita muscaria* or fly agaric mushroom has a vibrant, distinctive appearance with its white stem, bright red cap and white spots (left over from its universal veil, see p.19). The fly agaric is native to forested areas of the northern hemisphere and has been introduced widely through the southern hemisphere as well; this mushroom contains two neurotoxins, ibotenic acid and muscimol, that can act as both mild poisons and hallucinogens.

Just as psilocybin binds with serotonin receptors in the brain, muscimol mimics the neurotransmitter Gamma aminobutyric acid (GABA) and can cause a sedative effect that borders on hypnosis. Ibotenic acid and muscimol induce physical symptoms like nausea, trembling and sweating, along with psychological experiences such as hallucinations and sensations of invincibility. The combined effect? An altered physical and mental state that can feel like transcendence into a higher, more spiritual realm — or like communicating directly with gods or spirits.

MUSHROOMS IMMORTALIZED IN CAVE ART

The oldest evidence of magic mushroom use comes from Northern Australian cave paintings dating back to 10,000 BCE, which depict mushroom heads believed to symbolize the psychedelic properties of fungi. Mushrooms have nearly as long a legacy in Africa, where they appear in Algerian cave murals 7,000 to 9,000 years old. In these ancient images humans — likely shamans — dance while holding mushrooms, and more mushrooms emerge from their bodies. The fungi resemble the hallucinogenic *Psilocybe mairei* variety, and the clear connection between mushrooms and the human body could suggest the presence of a mushroom "cult" built around the psychedelic experience.

More ancient fungi artwork comes from the Selva Pascuala cave in Spain, where a 6,000-year-old painting depicts 13 small objects that resemble *Psilocybe hispanica* mushrooms native to the area. Like the Algerian images, this cave art suggests that its creators were aware of the fungi's mind-altering properties and may have incorporated them into spiritual beliefs.

MUSHROOMS IN MESOAMERICA

Moving forward in time from prehistoric cave art, we can find ample evidence of Psilocybe mushrooms' importance to Mesoamerican cultures, beginning with the Olmec and Mayan peoples. Archaeologists have uncovered Olmec and Mayan "mushroom stones" dating all the way back to 1,000 BCE — these stone carvings take the shape of a mushroom cap and stem and incorporate depictions of animals and people. Ancient Mayan Codices (books written on bark paper) include illustrations of mushrooms amid scenes of human sacrifice, while a mural in Teotihuacan, the largest urban settlement in pre-Aztec Mesoamerica, shows priests gathering Psilocybe mushrooms around the rain god Tlaloc.

Mayan and Olmec myths portray priests as humans who have special abilities to visit spiritual realms, where they ask the gods for bountiful harvests and cures for diseases. Psychedelic mushrooms, which alter and broaden sensory perception, would have proven an essential tool for these spiritual leaders.

Following the fall of the Mayan civilization, the Aztecs continued to display a special reverence for hallucinogenic mushrooms during their reign from the fourteenth to sixteenth centuries AD — and due to Spanish colonization of Central America, we have ample records of the Aztecs' mushroom use. Aztecs referred to Psilocybe mushrooms as *Teonanácatl*, or "god mushrooms", and relied on the fungi as a central aspect of spiritual rituals. One sixteenth-century Spanish missionary and ethnographer, Fray Bernardino de Sahagún, wrote that the Aztecs "who eat [mushrooms] see visions and feel fluttering of the heart." Another Spanish observer, the physician Francisco Hernández de Toledo, described magic mushrooms as creating "before the eyes all kinds of things, such as wars and the likeness of demons."

According to Spanish accounts, Aztecs who ingested psychedelic mushrooms would dance, weep or even run madly through the streets, and mushroom consumption often occurred alongside human sacrifice or ritual suicide.

Magic mushrooms feature prominently in Aztec art, such as an effigy of the Aztec flower god, Xochipilli, with Psilocybe mushroom caps on his knees and ears. Aztec myth claims that wherever the blood of the serpent god Quetzalcoatl spilled, magic mushrooms grew from the earth — and Quetzalcoatl schooled both humans and gods in the benefits of these "god mushrooms".

When ingesting hallucinogenic mushrooms, the ancient Mesoamerican people truly saw themselves as partaking of the flesh of the gods.

FUNGI IN THE FAR NORTH

Five-thousand years ago, on the other side of the Earth from Mesoamerica, Siberian shamanistic practices involving magic mushrooms emerged out of Paleolithic hunting societies. In particular, the Koryak tribe located near the Bering Sea used fly agaric mushrooms, which they gathered during the summer and dried to preserve for colder months. Fly agaric's psychedelic effects provided the Koryak an escape from long, cold winter nights of the north, and brought visions that they believed foretold the future.

Koryak folktales state that the first shaman, Big Raven, gained strength from fly agaric, and then ordered the fungi to grow abundantly so it might be used by humans. In many cases, dried fly agaric was so precious that only a shaman would ingest it, and the rest of the tribe would then drink the shaman's urine, with hallucinogenic qualities intact.

Reindeer living in Siberia enjoy the effects of fly agaric mushrooms — a fact that was well known to the Koryak. The tribespeople observed reindeer seeking out both the mushrooms themselves and the urine of humans who had consumed the fungi.

FROM MUSHROOMS TO SANTA CLAUS

Reindeer who ingested fly agaric would behave as if drunk, and perhaps snacked on the fungi to relieve the discomfort of a long winter just as humans did. Whatever the reason, the reindeer's preference became part of another folkloric tradition: the connection between fly agaric and Santa Claus.

A few scholars, such as Harvard's Donald Pfister, see a link between Santa Claus and Siberian shamans who brought dried fly agaric to villagers — carried in a cloth sack similar to Santa's — as a Winter Solstice gift. Snow often blocked the doors of village yurts, or huts, so shamans would enter through a hole in the roof where smoke escaped; a clear parallel to Santa coming down the chimney. Santa's red-and-white outfit mirrors the bright colours of the fly agaric. And as for those flying reindeer; well, they may simply be high on psychedelic mushrooms.

Even if these connections might be coincidental, they are rooted in real aspects of Siberian shamanism: shamans believed that animal spirits accompanied them on mushroom-aided, hallucinatory journeys. The idea of shamans leading reindeer across the sky, like Santa driving his sleigh, is not too far of a leap.

MUSHROOMS AND CHRISTMAS: A LONG-STANDING LINK

Centuries have passed since Siberian shamans offered mushroom gifts; however, fungi have become a lasting part of Christmas-themed culture and folklore throughout Europe and the US. As legends of Santa-like shamans spread across Northern Europe, people also noticed fly agaric mushrooms growing at the base of pine, fir and spruce trees. These elements likely combined to form the German tradition of hanging a red-and-white *glückspilz*, or "lucky mushroom" ornament, on the Christmas tree.

In France, Belgium and Switzerland, the traditional *bûche de Noël* cake often features red-and-white mushroom decorations. The log-shaped cake, like the mushrooms, is a nod to pagan celebrations of the Winter Solstice.

Fly agaric mushrooms also feature prominently in British and American Victorian-era Christmas cards, with images showing gnomes or elves in mushroom houses, and anthropomorphic, bearded mushrooms that resemble Santa himself.

SOMA: THE DIVINE MUSHROOM OF IMMORTALITY

In the period when Siberians used fly agaric in their spiritual rituals, the same mushroom may have been a key ingredient in religious rituals taking place among the Aryans of Central Asia, including what is now Iran and Afghanistan. A Hindu text known as the Rig Veda, dated from 1500 to 1200 BCE, describes Soma, a psychedelic substance that was also deified (portrayed as a god). When priests consumed a drink made from this hallucinogenic substance, the god Soma, giver of health and prosperity, was believed to appear before the Aryan people.

Scholars have disagreed over what the substance called Soma actually consisted of, but ethnomycologist R. Gordon Wasson, who studied the sociological influence of mushrooms, made a convincing case that Soma is fly agaric in his 1968 work *Soma: Divine Mushroom of Immortality.* Wasson points out that the Rig Veda depicts Soma as lacking leaves and having a thick stalk; the text does not mention seeds, roots or how to cultivate Soma, which suggests this "plant" may have been a mushroom.

THE ELEUSINIAN MYSTERIES: GODDESSES AND FUNGI

R. Gordon Wasson also proposed that mushrooms played a key part in the spiritual rituals of the Ancient Greeks, particularly the Eleusinian Mysteries practised from 16,000 BCE to 392 CE. These secret ceremonies, elements of which are portrayed on Greek pottery and paintings, were dedicated to the goddess Persephone.

The Eleusinian Mysteries honoured the cycle of the seasons by re-enacting Persephone's descent to the Underworld. Her descent marked the coming of winter aboveground, and her return to Earth that heralded the arrival of spring. During the ceremonies, initiates drank kykeon — a beverage believed to contain ergot, a psychedelic fungus that grows on barley. In his book *The Road to Eleusis*, Wasson and his co-authors suggested that ergot's hallucination-inducing compounds were an important part of the Greek's spiritual practices.

In what is now Spain, ergot remnants were discovered within an Eleusinian temple, both inside a vase and in the tooth tartar of human remains. Thus, archaeological evidence supports the hypothesis that the Greeks consumed psychedelic mushrooms during these rituals. The powers of fungi may well have helped the Greeks bring Persephone's journey to life.

MAGIC MUSHROOMS –
THE EGYPTIAN FOOD OF THE GODS

While the Greeks used barley-based ergot fungi, the ancient Egyptians also grew psychedelic mushrooms on barley — in the Egyptians' case, they cultivated a variety of Psilocybe fungi known as *Psilocybe cubensis*. Like the Aztecs, the Egyptians equated magic mushrooms with their gods: Egyptians believed hallucinogenic mushrooms were a gift from the god Osiris, and the Egyptian Book of the Dead describes mushrooms as both "the food of the gods" and "the flesh of the gods". As such, mushrooms were reserved for royalty and priests, and commoners were forbidden from consuming or even touching them.

Ancient Egyptian artwork and architecture reflects the culture's reverence for psychedelic mushrooms. Images of Psilocybes appear within hieroglyphic texts and on temple walls, such as a relief depicting a mushroom basket in the Temple of Hathor. Temple pillars themselves resemble mushroom stalks topped with giant caps. Some scholars have even suggested that the ankh, the Egyptian symbol of life, may depict a mushroom with a stem and rounded cap.

CELTIC MUSHROOM MAGIC

In the British Isles, the Celts also venerated mushrooms. Dating back over 2,400 years, Celtic culture relies on a deep connection with nature, including two magic mushrooms native to the British Isles: the fly agaric and a Psilocybe called the liberty cap, which resembles a tiny elf's hat.

Irish folklore is full of heroes who ingest strange plants — most likely mushrooms — and experience life-changing visions. In real life, high-ranking Celts known as druids consumed mushrooms to aid their spiritual journeys. The Celts understood that fungi grow out of a larger underground network and, by eating mushroom fruits, druids saw themselves as gaining access to that underground world — to the wisdom of their buried ancestors and of the Earth itself.

Some scholars suggest that psychedelic mushrooms influenced Celtic art, as the swirls and spirals of Celtic carvings resemble the distorted visions of a mushroom trip. Magic mushrooms are also deeply intertwined with Celtic fairy lore, with mushrooms and fairies going by the same slang term "pookie". In fact, the fairy-mushroom connection has persisted for centuries, as we'll see in our next section.

✳ MUSHROOMS AND FAIRY LORE: ✳ FROM THE CELTS TO THE VICTORIANS

A cornerstone of ancient Celtic beliefs was the idea of fairies as a mythical race of beings who were forced off the Earth and had to live underground. Celts also understood that mushrooms came from beneath the ground; therefore, ingesting mushrooms could strengthen humans' connection to these magical beings. Add in the fact that fly agaric and liberty caps produce hallucinations, and it's not surprising that Celts who took mushrooms would experience visions of the elves, gnomes and pixies so central to their worldview. In fact, people of the British Isles have long referred to psychedelic mushroom trips as "going away with the fairies".

When Celtic culture waned, fairy lore remained part of the British Isles, and so did the fairies' association with mushrooms. By the nineteenth century, the Victorians had embraced fairy art as a nostalgic reminder of a pre-industrial society bonded to nature. Images of fairies dancing among mushrooms, sitting on toadstool caps and using fungi as homes appeared everywhere — from greeting cards to children's illustrations to paintings by well-known artists like Richard Doyle and Walter Jenks Morgan.

FAIRY RINGS

One favourite subject of Victorian fairy art was fairy rings — the natural phenomenon of mushrooms springing up in a ringlike shape. Today, we understand that fairy rings occur because of mycelial growth underground. Mushroom fruiting bodies appear at the circular perimeter of the mycelium, where hyphae threads have reached fresh soil and absorbed the most nutrition.

In the past, however, fairy rings became centres of superstition. In the British Isles, the rings were believed both to be caused by dancing fairies, and to provide mushroom seats for fairies to rest between dances. Humans were warned to avoid fairy rings, lest they be drawn into the supernatural revelry and forced to dance to death.

Other countries developed similarly sinister stories: in Germany the rings were *Hexenridge,* or witches' rings, and in France *ronds de sorcières,* or witches' circles. These were thought to be dangerous spots where witches danced and cast spells. Austrian legends claimed that the rings were created by fiery dragon tails, while in Holland they marked spots where the Devil set down his milk churn.

All these legends reflect a reverence for the mysterious, possibly magical mushroom.

FROM MAGIC TO MEDICINE: MUSHROOMS IN THE EAST

So far, we've looked at cultures that valued mushrooms for their psychedelic properties and association with magical beings. However, in the East Asian cultures of China, Japan and Korea, mushrooms have been prized for centuries for a different reason: their medicinal and nutritional qualities. These benefits led to fungi becoming part of a quest for human immortality, and mushrooms themselves being immortalized in ancient art.

MUSHROOMS IN ANCIENT CHINA

The first definitive mentions of mushrooms in Chinese history occur during the Han dynasty of 206 BCE to 220 CE. During this period, a compilation called the Book of Songs recorded folk songs, poems and descriptions of edible and medicinal plants — including mushrooms.

Also, during the Han dynasty, many Taoists attempted to create "elixirs of immortality" that they hoped would grant them eternal life and health. Medicinal mushrooms may have been among the ingredients in these potions, with one Han dynasty poem describing a "stone mushroom" and "magic fungus" found on the legendary Islands of the Immortals.

LINGZHI: THE MUSHROOM OF IMMORTALITY

The "magic fungus" mentioned during the Han dynasty may well be lingzhi, or *Ganoderma Lucidum,* more commonly known in the West as reishi. Lingzhi, the fungi's traditional Chinese name, translates to "divine mushroom", and it was revered throughout ancient China as the "mushroom of immortality". Chinese medical texts from as early as 502 CE reference lingzhi's power to reduce aging, increase energy, and improve memory and heart health; by the Ming dynasty in 1590 CE, lingzhi was featured in China's first pharmacopeia.

Adding to lingzhi's mystique was the fact that it grew so scarcely, and was believed to appear only at sacred spiritual sites in the mountains. By ingesting these medicinal mushrooms, the Chinese saw themselves as not only improving their physical health, but also connecting to the natural world and spiritual realms. Chinese art reflects this link between the medicinal, the natural and the divine. Sixteenth-century silk art shows lingzhi being offered as a gift to a mother goddess, while in an eighteenth-century painting, a god known as the Divine Farmer holds a basket of lingzhi he has foraged.

MUSHROOMS IN JAPAN:
ART, MEDICINE AND RELIGION

Mushrooms have been part of Japanese culture since ancient times. Ceramic mushrooms were discovered at a 4,000-year-old Japanese archaeological site, and mushrooms are an important ingredient in Japanese Buddhist temple food, known as *shōjin ryōri* or "devotion cuisine". Vegetarianism is a part of Buddhism's policy of non-violence, so mushrooms' meaty flavour and texture has proved a valuable meat substitute. One highly nutritious mushroom, shiitake, was so important to the Buddhists of feudal Japan that they would only build temples where this species was plentiful.

Mushrooms play a key role in ancient Japanese medicine, or *kampo*. Medical mushrooms such as maitake were so prized by the Japanese that the kanji symbol for "maitake" combines the glyph for "dance" and "mushroom" — because one would literally dance with joy upon finding this rare mushroom with its healing powers.

Mushrooms also appear in traditional Japanese art, as miniature sculptures called *netsuke*, and in contemporary pop art. Yayoi Kusama created giant polka-dotted mushroom sculptures, while Takashi Murakami paints mushrooms covered with wide eyes and psychedelic patterns.

MUSHROOMS OF LONG LIFE IN KOREA

From the fifth century onward, mushrooms were one of ten longevity symbols, or *ship-jangsaeng*, included on Korean paintings, ceramics and tapestries. The *ship-jangsaeng* appeared everywhere from *minhwa,* folk art produced by commoners, to elite tombs of the Goryeo and Joseon dynasties.

Korean longevity mushrooms were of the same *Ganoderma lucidum* species so prized in China, but in Korea they were known as *yeongji*, or mushrooms of eternal youth and long life. According to Korean legend, the *yeongji* could only be found by phoenix, deer and cranes — the latter two animals also among the *ship-jangsaeng* symbols.

Depictions of mushrooms are plentiful in Buddhist temples where the Hwarang, traditional Korean martial artists, lived and studied for centuries. The Hwarang may have received their knowledge of mushrooms' healing and energizing power from the Mudang, Korean shamans who were predominantly female. Throughout Korean history, the Hwarang protected the Mudang from invaders such as the Japanese, and in turn the Mudang shared their healing wisdom with the Hwarang warriors.

BETWEEN THE EAST AND WEST: MUSHROOMS IN RUSSIA

The Russian people have historically valued mushrooms not as medicines or psychedelics, but simply as sources of culinary delight. Russians traditionally taught their children how to forage for mushrooms in the woods from a young age, and mushroom picking is a central pastime in Russian culture.

Russian ethnomycologist Valentina Pavlovna — wife of R. Gordon Wasson (see p.52) — co-wrote *Mushrooms, Russia and History* with her husband. Pavlovna wrote that mushroom foraging connected her, like many Russian children throughout history, to the riches of the natural world. She suggested that Russians have a particular devotion to mushrooms that few other cultures share; for her people, mushrooms are the bountiful fruit of "Mother Russia". They are a valuable source of nutrition and culinary variety, a food that can be found in the wild, dried and preserved for the winter months. These fungi form the basis of hearty stews, soups and stroganoff dishes.

For the Russians, mushrooms are a true source of sustenance and even joy. They have made their way into Russian folklore, with fungi appearing in stories and artwork of the powerful Russian witch Baba Yaga.

Mushroom foraging has influenced many popular Russian proverbs, such as: "Without stooping down for the mushroom, you cannot put it in your basket." A Russian nursery rhyme called "Panic Among the Mushrooms" describes a mushroom captain trying to convince different mushroom species to follow him into battle — thus transferring knowledge of fungi to new generations as part of a bedtime story.

Mushrooms also make frequent appearances in Russian literature, including works by Tolstoy, Pushkin and Gogol. In *Anna Karenina*, a character considers proposing while mushroom foraging with his lover.

In fact, fungi can be found in literature and popular culture from many countries — and we'll examine some of these mushroom legacies in the final section of this chapter.

✳ MUSHROOMS IN LITERATURE ✳ AND POPULAR CULTURE

Mushrooms have appeared in literature as far back as Shakespeare. In *The Tempest,* Prospero addresses the faeries as "you whose pastime/Is to make midnight mushrooms" — a clear nod to the fairy-mushroom connection. In 1864, Jules Verne imagined a forest of gigantic mushrooms in his science-fiction classic *A Journey to the Centre of the Earth.* Another of the first science fiction authors, H. G. Wells, wrote about hallucinogenic and poisonous mushrooms in his 1896 story *The Purple Pileus.*

Children's author and naturalist Beatrix Potter, creator of the character Peter Rabbit, also took an interest in mushrooms. Potter produced detailed botanical illustrations of fungi in the 1800s.

Perhaps the most famous mushroom in literature occurs in a children's fantasy novel, *Alice's Adventures in Wonderland*, published in 1865. This tale by Lewis Carroll has been retold and referenced to become a lasting part of British and American popular culture. While we don't know if Carroll had magic mushrooms in mind, the parallel to psychedelic mushroom use is hard to deny.

In *Alice's Adventures in Wonderland*, Alice encounters a talking caterpillar perched atop a mushroom. The caterpillar tells Alice that if she eats the mushroom "one side will make you grow taller, and the other side will make you grow shorter." Clearly, Carroll's mushroom distorts perception just like real hallucinogenic fungi. The rest of the novel, in which Alice continues to eat mushroom pieces before encountering bizarre creatures and places, could be read as one wild mushroom trip.

Disney has made multiple movies of Alice's trippy story, and mushrooms also feature in another of Disney's visually inventive works, *Fantasia*. In the film, red-capped mushrooms that resemble fly agarics dance to the music of Tchaikovsky.

A more recent example of mushroom-infused pop culture is Nintendo's Super Mario Brothers video game. The game takes place in a Mushroom Kingdom, and the characters ingest red-and-white Super Mushrooms that make them larger — not unlike Alice's mushroom, and not unlike the fly agaric with its ability to alter our perceptions of size and scale.

As our knowledge of and interest in mushrooms continues to grow, we can expect to find fungi popping up in even more of our art and entertainment.

CHAPTER 5

IDENTIFYING MUSHROOMS

In this chapter, you'll learn about common mushrooms of the northern hemisphere that you can search for on your own. Now, let's get ready to find and identify some mushrooms!

Please note this information is meant for observation only. As so many poisonous mushrooms appear similar to edible species, picking and eating mushrooms found in the wild is always a risk.

PREPARING FOR A MUSHROOM HUNT

1. **Find the Right Time** – the best time to search for mushrooms is in the days following heavy rain, when the moist ground encourages mushroom fruit bodies to emerge. As for time of year, most mushrooms fruit in autumn, although some appear in spring and a few in summer or winter. If you want to find specific mushrooms, it's worth looking up growing patterns in your specific climate.

2. **Find the Right Place** – mushrooms typically grow in wooded areas. If you can't make it to a forest, you can always keep an eye out around trees or fallen logs in your neighbourhood – you may find treasure close to home! Mushrooms can also appear around compost piles or in your garden. Anywhere mycelium has decayed plant matter to feed on, a mushroom can sprout up.

3. **Wear the Right Clothing** – if you plan on getting close to mushrooms to observe them, you may have to stray off the path and into bushes and brambles. Long sleeves, trousers and hiking boots are preferable, as well as sunscreen and a hat.

CONSIDER A MUSHROOM JOURNAL

If hunting for mushrooms without picking them seems like a disappointment, consider creating a lasting record of your mushroom search: a mushroom journal. You can carry a small journal and pencil with you on hikes, note which mushrooms you found in which locations, and even try your hand at botanical illustrations. You'll be following in the footsteps of author and illustrator Beatrix Potter, whom we mentioned in our previous chapter. A dedicated mushroom forager, Potter drew over 350 accurate depictions of fungi. Her illustrations have appeared in scientific publications and are exhibited in art galleries to this day.

In our modern era, smartphone cameras provide another way to keep track of your fungal finds.

If you find yourself mushroom hunting over several years, your journal may prove particularly useful: thanks to underground mycelial growth, mushrooms will often pop up again in the same places they did in previous seasons. Keeping track of your discoveries could come in handy for future hunts!

MUSHROOM HUNT RESPONSIBLY

We've learned about the crucial role fungi play in protecting the forest ecosystem, so, while searching for mushrooms, it's important to respect both fungi themselves and the rest of the natural world. Heavy trampling can destroy immature mushroom fruit bodies before they have a chance to spread spores and may damage the mycelium beneath the earth. Disturbing dead leaves could mean scattering a growing mushroom's environment, so be sure to tread lightly.

And, of course, one should tread lightly in a figurative sense as well. Avoid harming plants, intruding on animals' habitats or leaving litter behind.

Now that we've got the basics covered, read on for a guide to some of the most interesting mushrooms in the northern hemisphere.

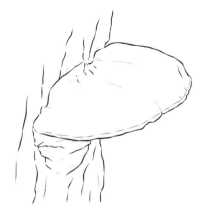

ARTIST'S CONK
GANODERMA APPLANATUM

HOW TO IDENTIFY:

Artist's conk grows in fan-shaped, stemless horizontal protrusions out of tree trunks, either singly or in groups. The fruiting bodies can range from just a few centimetres in size, to up to 30 centimetres wide, 50 centimetres long and 10 centimetres thick. Artist's conk has thick, leatherlike flesh, and the brown, wrinkled upper surface contains ridges that indicate each new year's growth, much like tree rings. The underside, however, is very different: smooth, white or tan, it's lined with barely detectable pores. This hidden side provides a perfect surface for etching out images.

WHEN AND WHERE TO FIND IT:

Artist's conk is very common across North America, the British Isles and most of mainland Europe. The fungi grows on hardwood and coniferous trees and can appear both on living tree trunks and fallen logs and stumps. Amazingly, fruiting bodies of this species can live for decades, so the artist's conk can be found at any time of year.

HISTORY AND USES:

Artist's conk is named for its ability to act as a canvas for creating art: When images are etched into the mushroom's underside with a sharp object or fingernail, the etchings appear in a darker brown shade than the general surface, almost like a tattoo. This colour change occurs because of pressure placed on the mushroom, so altering the pressure while drawing can cause a chiaroscuro effect, with varying shades of light and dark. Humans have etched images onto artist's conk for centuries.

Artist's conk is also used medicinally as a tea or powder; studies show this species supports immune health and may even fight cancer.

CHANTERELLE
CANTHARELLUS CIBARIUS

HOW TO IDENTIFY:

Chanterelles are egg-yolk-coloured mushrooms shaped like a goblet or funnel. The fungi's fluted surface is smooth on the inside, while horizontal folds line the outside, running down to the stem. Their caps range from 5 to 13 centimetres in diameter, with a thin stalk the size of a finger, and they sometimes smell like apricots. To distinguish chanterelles from similar species, look for folds rather than gills, as true chanterelles do not have gills. In addition, the outer surface of chanterelles is uniform in colour, rather than growing darker toward the centre of the mushroom. When split open, chanterelles are white on the inside, and they grow as individual mushrooms on the forest floor, rather than in connected clumps.

WHEN AND WHERE TO FIND IT:

Chanterelles grow throughout the United States and Europe in coniferous, beech and birch forests and among grasses and herbs. They are also native to Africa and Asia. In Britain these fungi appear from midsummer until the end of December; in the eastern US they grow in summer and autumn, while on the west coast they pop up in autumn, winter and spring.

HISTORY AND USES:

Chanterelles have been considered a gourmet delicacy for centuries and were served to French royalty in the 1700s. The chanterelle's rich, unique taste, sometimes referred to as fruity, peppery or even flowerlike, is frequently used in sautés, creamy sauces and soups. This mushroom is particularly common in the Pacific Northwest, and it ranks as Oregon's official state mushroom.

CHICKEN OF THE WOODS
LAETIPORUS SULPHUREUS

HOW TO IDENTIFY:

Chicken of the woods grow in horizontal shelves out of tree trunks. These fungi are a bright yellow-orange colour, and the undersides of their caps are lined with tiny spore-producing pores. The caps have a rippled, uneven surface, and their fanlike shapes are between 5 and 25 centimetres wide and 3 centimetres thick.

WHEN AND WHERE TO FIND IT:

In North America, chicken of the woods is only commonly found to the east of the Rocky Mountains. The species grows widely all over the United Kingdom, Europe and northern Asia. It most commonly grows on oak, sweet chestnut, willow, yew and beech trees during spring and autumn, and it often reappears in the same spot every year — so if you find some, definitely note the location in your foraging journal!

HISTORY AND USES:

Chicken of the woods is best known for sharing its flavour and texture with chicken. It's considered a gourmet mushroom and can be grilled or fried just like real meat. In European countries such as Germany, a powder made of dried chicken of the woods is mixed with flour to bake bread. However, chicken of the woods can also be seen as a pest, as it causes heart rot by eating out the centres of trees. In the past, this mushroom frequently damaged the British Navy's wooden ships.

DEATH CAP
AMANITA PHALLOIDES

HOW TO IDENTIFY:

The death cap has a rounded or flattened cap of 5 to 15 centimetres in diameter, which can be white, yellow, pale green, olive or brown in colour. Many white gills crowd close together beneath the cap. This mushroom grows out of the ground with a stem longer than the cap is wide, and has a skirt-like ring around the stalk. One of death cap's most reliable identifiers is the white cup holding the base of the stem, but this attribute can often be hidden beneath the earth or debris. This mushroom can have a honey-like smell when immature, but a fully grown specimen will emit a foul, overbearingly sweet scent.

WHEN AND WHERE TO FIND IT:

The death cap is found widely throughout Europe, particularly in the British Isles, often beneath oak, beech, pine, spruce, birch and chestnut trees. While this mushroom is not native to North America, it has been introduced to the US alongside imported species like chestnut trees, and is most common along both coastlines. The mushrooms generally fruit in summer and autumn, but appear in winter in the western US. These fungi are safe to touch — the poison is contained within the mushroom flesh and can't be absorbed through human skin — it is better to appreciate this mushroom from a distance!

HISTORY AND USES:

The death cap has been well known since Greek and Roman times as the world's deadliest mushroom, containing amatoxins that will cause what first resembles a case of food poisoning, but can go on to cause fatal liver and kidney damage. Despite — or, rather, because of — the death cap's dangerous qualities, humans have made use of this mushroom throughout history: many believe that Roman Empress Agrippina used this mushroom to poison her husband, the Emperor Claudius. The Holy Roman Emperor Charles VI may also have been poisoned by death cap in 1740.

FLY AGARIC
AMANITA MUSCARIA

HOW TO IDENTIFY:

The fly agaric is immediately identifiable through its bright red cap and tiny white spots, which are left over from the mushroom's universal veil. However, a few species have yellow or white caps. This species is a classic toadstool mushroom, with its rounded cap of 8 to 20 centimetres wide and gills on its underside. It rises from a stalk of 10 to 25 centimetres that includes a grooved ring, another remnant of the universal veil.

WHEN AND WHERE TO FIND IT:

Fly agaric grows throughout temperate and boreal woodlands of the northern hemisphere, encompassing Europe, northern Asia and North America. These mushrooms are often found near the base of birch, pine and spruce trees, and they form fruiting bodies from late summer to early winter.

HISTORY AND USES:

Fly agaric is considered a poisonous mushroom because its chemical compounds, ibotenic acid and muscimol, can cause nausea, vomiting and seizures. However, it rarely causes lasting illness or death, and humans have purposefully ingested fly agaric for centuries because of those same chemical compounds — as they also cause hallucinations. Ancient civilizations including the Celts and Siberians employed fly agaric as part of spiritual rituals, which we covered in Chapter Four of this book. Fly agaric has also become a widespread cultural symbol, appearing everywhere from Christmas decorations to fairy art to the video game Super Mario Brothers.

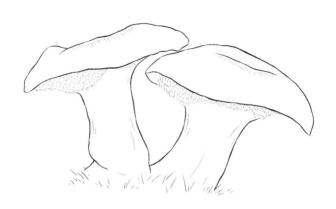

HEDGEHOG
HYDNUM REPANDUM

HOW TO IDENTIFY:

The hedgehog mushroom is named for the tiny hedgehog-like spikes hidden beneath the surface of the mushroom cap. These fungi range in colour from brown to yellow or orange, and the flattened, uneven cap spans up to 17 centimetres wide. The spikes beneath the cap — which also serve as spore-release mechanisms — are only 2 to 7 millimetres long. The 3-to-10-centimetre stalk is sometimes off-centre, adding to its uneven appearance. The hedgehog has a brittle texture, which separates it from other spiked mushrooms — other varieties have leathery, hard-to-break flesh.

WHEN AND WHERE TO FIND IT:

Hedgehog mushrooms are among the most common of the "tooth fungi" — so called for their toothlike spikes — throughout Europe and North America. They typically fruit between summer and autumn, although they can appear throughout winter in the US, west of the Rockies. Hedgehog fungi appear on the ground in coniferous and deciduous forests, individually or in small groups rather than a larger clumping.

HISTORY AND USES:

Hedgehog mushrooms are edible and used in French, Italian and Spanish cuisine; their flavour is sweet and nutty, and their flesh absorbs liquids and takes on the taste of ingredients they are prepared with. The more vibrantly coloured hedgehogs are used to dye wool in Norway.

HEN OF THE WOODS
GRIFOLA FRONDOSA

HOW TO IDENTIFY:

Hen of the woods grows in clusters at the base of trees and resembles a pile of leaves, or a grouping of overlapping feathers like those on a hen. The upper surface of the mushroom is a grey to brown shade, with white or yellow pores on the underside, and the entire cluster is about the size of a melon. These groupings can weigh as little as 2 kilograms, or as much as 22 kilograms!

WHEN AND WHERE TO FIND IT:

Hen of the woods mainly appears at the base of oak trees, although it can be found near other deciduous trees as well. This mushroom grows in the UK, northern Europe, the northeastern US and Asia. Hen of the woods fruits from late summer through the autumn, and fruiting bodies typically reappear in the same spot every year.

HISTORY AND USES:

In Japan, hen of the woods is known as maitake, the highly valued medicinal mushroom we learned about in Chapter Four. This mushroom was used to strengthen the immune system in traditional Japanese medicine, and in our modern era it has been found to have anti-HIV properties. Hen of the woods is also an edible mushroom popular for its meat-like texture.

LION'S MANE
HERICIUM ERINACEUS

HOW TO IDENTIFY:

Lion's mane is one of the most striking mushrooms, with its 1-to-5-centimetre-long dangling spines that cover the entire surface of the mushroom. These fungi truly do resemble a lion's mane or, as some of its other common names imply, an "old-man's beard", "Santa's beard", "deer's tail" or even "pom-pom". The mushroom grows out of live or dead trees and has no stem, and the spines first appear as a bright white that yellows as the fungi ages. Most lion's manes are 10 to 25 centimetres wide, and can be rounded or elongated in shape.

WHEN AND WHERE TO FIND IT:

Lion's mane grows plentifully in North America, Europe and Asia. In warmer climates it can be found in autumn, winter and spring, while in chillier climates it appears only in summer and autumn. Because lion's mane feeds on dead wood from live or dead trees, it is often found on species including oaks, beeches, maples, sycamores and conifers. Lion's mane generally appears in a single clump high above ground level, unless it is growing out of a felled log.

HISTORY AND USES:

Lion's mane is a staple of traditional Eastern medicine, where it has been used for centuries to boost memory and brain health, improve overall immune health and reduce inflammation. Buddhist monks took lion's mane to help focus during meditation, and in modern times lion's mane has become a popular supplement to aid cognitive function and concentration. Scientific research has identified this mushroom as a promising treatment for dementia and other neurological diseases, in part because it stimulates growth and repair of nerve cells.

MOREL

MORCHELLA ESCULENTA

HOW TO IDENTIFY:

Morels are brownish-grey mushrooms whose caps contain ridges and craters, creating a honeycomb-like texture. Their bulb or cone-shaped caps are about 2 to 7 centimetres wide and rise above a 2-to-9-centimetre stem. Morels are hollow inside, unlike some similar mushrooms that are solid. In addition, morels do not have a ring around their stalks.

WHEN AND WHERE TO FIND IT:

Morels grow in the spring, after the last frost, and often after a significant rainfall. Morels are found throughout the United States and Europe but are less common in the UK compared to countries like France, Italy and Germany. These fungi tend to appear at the bases of trees, particularly aspen, oak, elm, ash, tulip poplars, apple trees and conifers.

HISTORY AND USES:

Studies of morel DNA reveal that this fungus has existed since the Cretaceous period, and its makeup hasn't changed much since that era. These mushrooms are culinary delicacies that feature widely in French cuisine; they have a nutty, earthy taste and are meaty but tender.

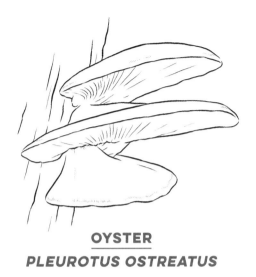

OYSTER
PLEUROTUS OSTREATUS

HOW TO IDENTIFY:

Oyster mushroom caps are shaped like the molluscs they are named after. Usually white, grey or tan in colour, the caps range from 2 to 30 centimetres in diameter, with gills beneath the cap's surface and continuing down to the 1-to-3-centimetre stem. These mushrooms grow on deciduous tree trunks or stumps and often cluster together in football-sized groupings. More unusual species include the golden and pink oyster mushrooms, with caps shaded to match their names.

WHEN AND WHERE TO FIND IT:

Oyster mushrooms can be found in subtropical and temperate forests nearly worldwide, though they do not grow in the Pacific Northwest of the United States and Canada. This hardy species forms fruiting bodies year-round, even in the snow! However, oyster mushrooms grow only on deciduous trees, so any similar mushroom on a coniferous tree is a possibly poisonous lookalike.

HISTORY AND USES:

Oyster mushrooms were first commercially cultivated in Germany during World War One, where the easy-to-grow mushrooms helped to combat food shortages. They have since become among the most widely grown mushrooms, with a mildly earthy taste, and are especially popular in Asian cuisine. Oyster mushrooms are also used in bioremediation — i.e. to eat up and neutralize pollutants. As we discussed in Chapter Three, these mushrooms have helped clean up oil spills and toxic ash from forest fires.

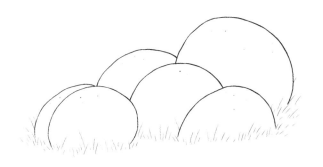

PUFFBALL

CALVATIA, CALBOVISTA, AND *LYCOPERDON* SPECIES

HOW TO IDENTIFY:

Puffball mushrooms generally have a smooth white surface, although some are lined with a darker fuzz or small, soft spikes. They form a simple ball shape with no cap, stem or gills. The *Calvatia* and *Calbovista* types can grow as wide as 1.5 metres, while *Lycoperdon* species can be grape-sized miniatures. Very few other mushrooms resemble the capless white puffball, so these fungi are some of the easiest to pinpoint in the wild. However, if the flesh inside is not a solid white, that's a sign that you may have found a poisonous mushroom instead.

WHEN AND WHERE TO FIND IT:

Puffball mushrooms can be found throughout the northern hemisphere, typically from late summer to autumn, although they grow from winter to spring in the western United States. Puffballs thrive in grassy areas like fields and meadows, and they're especially abundant in well-fertilized lawns and golf courses.

HISTORY AND USES:

Humans have both eaten and used puffball mushrooms medicinally for centuries. A number of Native American tribes, including the Navajo and Chippewa, made a paste of puffball spores and applied it to wounds to staunch bleeding. The Cherokee used puffballs to heal burns and colonizing settlers absorbed their knowledge. Many Native American tribes also ate puffballs, and in both England and the US, humans burned puffballs because the smoke calmed bees and allowed them to harvest honey. Tibetans have also traditionally burned puffballs, but for a different reason: they used the mushroom ash to make ink.

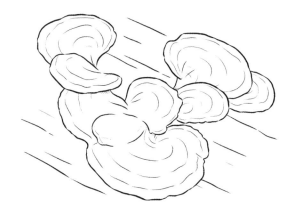

REISHI
GANODERMA LUCIDUM

HOW TO IDENTIFY:

Reishi mushrooms grow out of tree stumps or trunks in a fan-like shape; their reddish-orange caps have a uniquely shiny, almost varnished appearance. A white to yellow margin surrounds the red portion of the cap as the mushroom is growing. Immature mushrooms also contain a small stem that disappears when the fungi is fully grown. Reishi can be as large as a dinner plate, but are usually between 10 and 15 centimetres wide and 1 to 3 centimetres thick.

WHEN AND WHERE TO FIND IT:

Reishi grow throughout North America, Europe and Asia and generally appear on hardwood or evergreen trees. They prefer warmer growing conditions and are easiest to find in summer and autumn, but some are hardy enough to last all year. Although they grow on trees, you might spot reishi on the ground where a tree stump has rotted away.

HISTORY AND USES:

In Chapter Four, we learned that the reishi is an important element of Chinese, Japanese and Korean culture and medicine. The mushroom's impressive health benefits have led to it being called the "mushroom of immortality", and it has appeared in Asian paintings, poems and folklore throughout history. Modern research backs up the reishi's benefits: it contains polysaccharides, peptidoglycans and triterpenoids that have powerful effects on the human body. These include boosting the activity of white blood cells that fight cancer, inhibiting tumour growth and encouraging liver health. Today, reishi are sold widely as a health supplement around the world.

TURKEY TAIL
TRAMETES VERSICOLOR

HOW TO IDENTIFY:

The turkey tail's Latin name includes the description *versicolor*, or "several colours". This mushroom is indeed marked by concentric circles of different colours, from white to yellow to orange, brown to red, blue to green, all lining its cap. Add in the half-circle, fan-like shape of the cap, and it truly resembles a turkey's tail. These fungi have no stalk, and the flat cap of 2.5 to 10 centimetres grows directly out of tree trunks, stumps and fallen branches. Turkey tail often grows in layers like tiles, and the underside contains tiny pores. Any similar-looking species with completely smooth undersides is not true turkey tail.

WHEN AND WHERE TO FIND IT:

Turkey tail grows in deciduous and coniferous forests all around the world. Because they are so long-lasting, they can be found at any time of year. Look for them on fallen tree logs or stumps.

HISTORY AND USES:

Turkey tail has long been prized as a medicinal mushroom in Asian medicine, and modern research has supported the species' health benefits. Turkey tail contains a molecule called polysaccharide K that strengthens the immune system, has antioxidant and antitumour properties, and is even a medically approved cancer treatment in Japan. Throughout the world, turkey tail is taken medicinally in teas, tinctures and supplements. However, turkey tail has a very tough texture and is not generally consumed outside of its medicinal use.

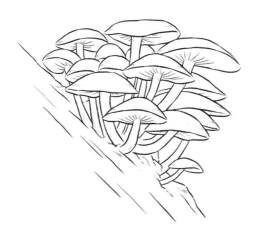

VELVET FOOT

FLAMMULINA VELUTIPES

HOW TO IDENTIFY:

The velvet foot is a deep orange or caramel-brown in colour, with a round cap 1 to 7 centimetres wide and a stalk shorter than a finger. The mushroom's name comes from the dark brown to black, velvet-textured hairs on the bottom of its stalk, which are absent in poisonous lookalike species. Velvet foot grows individually or in clumps on trees, occasionally beneath peeling bark or in hollows within tree trunks.

WHEN AND WHERE TO FIND IT:

Velvet foot grows on hardwood trees and is common on elm, beech, ash and oaks. It grows throughout the British Isles, mainland Europe, and North America from autumn through to early spring. Velvet foot is also known as the "winter mushroom" because it fruits even in the coldest, snowiest winter months. A snowy day is a great time to search for velvet foot, since its orange-brown shade will stand out like "little flames" — as its Latin name, *Flammulina,* suggests.

HISTORY AND USES:

Velvet foot is most popular in Japan, where it has been cultivated for hundreds of years; however, this human-grown version looks completely different from the wild mushroom. The Japanese refer to this mushroom as "enokitake" and grow it in jars in the dark — a high-carbon-dioxide environment that coaxes the fungi to fruit in long, thin white stalks topped with tiny white caps. In Japan, enokitake are the basis for a widespread condiment called nametake. These fungi are also known to ease intestinal and liver issues in traditional Asian medicine.

CHAPTER 6

MUSHROOM RECIPES

After reading about and searching for so many fascinating mushrooms, you've likely worked up quite an appetite. The good news is that many mushroom varieties are readily available at your local supermarket, and provide the perfect basis for nutritious, delicious meals. In this chapter, you'll learn how to make appetizers, main and side dishes, and even a dessert featuring a variety of different mushrooms. After all you've read, you'll know that preparing and eating mushrooms connects you to rich cultural and environmental legacies and provides many health benefits as well.

A WORD ON USING DRIED MUSHROOMS

Adding dried mushrooms to your cooking routine is a great way to enjoy multiple species of mushrooms all year long, and keep them on hand in your pantry. It allows you to procure fungi that are harder to find fresh, such as morels and chanterelles — you can buy these varieties dried online, in gourmet shops and at many supermarkets. For the best quality, your safest bet is to purchase mushrooms from high-end, organic grocers or online retailers that specialize in mushrooms. Do research before buying, as some mushrooms imported from Asia have been found to contain high levels of pesticides or chemicals from pollution. And if you have the chance to inspect your mushrooms in person, choose mushrooms that aren't shrivelled, broken, or full of holes — which could indicate insects snacked on them!

Once you're ready to use your dried mushrooms, preparing them is simple. Just rinse the dried mushrooms in cold water, drain and air-dry. Then pour hot water over the mushrooms until completely covered and let sit for up to 30 minutes, or until soft. Drain, rinse and use anywhere you would fresh mushrooms.

CONVERSIONS AND MEASUREMENTS

The recipes in this chapter use metric measurements, but if you prefer using imperial (and you don't have a smartphone to do the conversions for you), here are some basic tables:

Grams to ounces
25 g ≈ 1 oz
60 g ≈ 2 oz
85 g ≈ 3 oz
115 g ≈ 4 oz
255 g ≈ 9 oz

Millilitres to fluid ounces
15 ml ≈ 0.5 fl. oz
30 ml ≈ 1 fl. oz
75 ml ≈ 2.5 fl. oz
120 ml ≈ 4 fl. oz
270 ml ≈ 9 fl. oz

CHINESE BUTTON MUSHROOM SOUP

(makes 4 servings)

This simple soup consists mainly of ingredients you're likely to have on hand, and is perfect to whip up for a warming snack or light meal.

INGREDIENTS

225 g chestnut mushrooms
2 tbsp sesame oil
1 ½ tsp soy sauce
Salt, to taste
4 tbsp coriander, finely chopped
1 spring onion, chopped

METHOD

Clean mushrooms. Place soup pot or large saucepan over medium heat, add oil and soy sauce to mushrooms, cup-side up, and cook until browned without stirring. Add 1 litre of water, bring to a boil, cover and simmer 5 minutes on low heat. Add salt to taste, stir in coriander and spring onion and serve.

MINI CHANTERELLE TOASTS

(makes 18 toasts)

These toasts are a great way to highlight chanterelle's distinctive peppery flavour. If you can't find fresh chanterelle at a speciality grocer or a farmer's market, you can use dried chanterelle or substitute a different mushroom — dried morels are another good choice. You could even make a few batches of toast featuring different fungi!

INGREDIENTS

225 g fresh or reconstituted chanterelle or assorted mushrooms

4 tbsp extra-virgin olive oil

1 bunch of chives (about 4 tbsp), finely chopped

2 tsp fresh rosemary, chopped

2 tsp fresh thyme, chopped

Salt

120 g sour cream

Fresh-ground black pepper

18 slices of baguette, about 1 cm thick

3 tbsp Parmesan cheese, grated

METHOD

Clean mushrooms and cut into 2–3 cm pieces. Preheat grill to high.

Heat 2 tbsp oil in a sauté pan over medium-high heat, add mushrooms and a pinch of salt, stir and cook 5 to 8 minutes or until browned. Remove mushrooms from heat, let cool and chop.

Return pan to medium heat, add remaining oil and cook chives, rosemary, thyme, and a pinch of salt until tender, 1 to 3 minutes. Add mushrooms, sour cream, and pepper, heat and stir.

Arrange baguette slices on a baking sheet, brush with olive oil, and toast under grill for 1 minute before flipping to toast other side for an additional minute. Top toast with warm mushroom mixture, sprinkle with Parmesan, and serve.

STUFFED MUSHROOM CAPS

(makes 12 caps)

These savoury, bite-size caps make a great party appetizer.

INGREDIENTS

12 large white mushrooms
8 tbsp extra-virgin olive oil
2 tbsp red bell pepper, finely chopped
3 tbsp onion, finely chopped
2 tbsp sun-dried tomato, finely chopped
60 g fresh breadcrumbs
½ tsp salt
Black pepper
4 tbsp Parmesan cheese, grated

METHOD

Preheat oven to 160°C (320°F). Clean mushrooms and remove stems, leaving caps whole. Finely chop stems.

Heat 4 tbsp olive oil in sauté pan and cook mushroom caps until tender, about 6 to 10 minutes. Set aside.

Place remaining olive oil in pan and sauté mushroom stems, bell pepper, and onion until onions are translucent, about 10 minutes. Add tomatoes, breadcrumbs, salt and pepper, stir and remove from heat.

Fill mushroom caps with breadcrumb-onion mixture, then sprinkle with Parmesan cheese.

Arrange mushroom caps on a buttered or parchment-lined baking dish, and bake 15 to 20 minutes or until cheese is melted and filling is browned.

Can be served hot or at room temperature.

You can also make this into a main dish by using larger portobello mushrooms!

MAIN DISHES

OYSTER MUSHROOM STIR-FRY

(serves 4)

With their meaty texture, oyster mushrooms make a great meat substitute in this recipe. You can also add other vegetables that catch your fancy, or try shiitake mushrooms instead.

INGREDIENTS

225 g fresh oyster or shiitake mushrooms, or reconstituted dry

2 tbsp sesame oil

90 g carrots, grated

6 spring onions, chopped

4 baby bok choy, leaves separated

3 tbsp soy sauce

1 tbsp black bean sauce

225 g dried egg noodles, cooked and drained

2 tbsp sesame seeds

METHOD

Cut oyster mushrooms away from firm central stem and discard stem (or, if using shiitake, slice mushrooms).

Heat oil in wok over medium-high heat and stir-fry mushrooms for 7 to 10 minutes, or until golden brown. Add carrots and spring onions and cook for one minute. Add bok choy and cook for an additional minute, until wilted. Add soy sauce, bean sauce and noodles, and stir until warmed through. Garnish with sesame seeds and serve.

You can add cubed tofu or cooked chicken if you need a heartier main dish!

MEATLESS LOAF

(serves 6)

This *meatless* version of meatloaf relies on button mushrooms for its texture and flavour.

INGREDIENTS

Butter, to grease loaf pan
1 onion, chopped
1 tbsp extra-virgin olive oil
170 g button mushrooms, sliced
80 g fresh breadcrumbs
1 egg, beaten
400 g canned chopped tomatoes
1 tbsp fresh thyme, chopped
1 tbsp fresh rosemary, chopped
2 tbsp tomato paste
Salt and pepper, to taste

METHOD

Preheat oven to 180°C (350°F). Grease a 23 × 14 cm loaf pan with butter, and sauté onion in olive oil over medium heat until softened, 5 to 10 minutes.

Combine all ingredients in a large bowl, or mix in a food processor. Place mixture in loaf pan and bake until solid and crispy on top — about 1 hour. Let sit for 15 minutes before unmoulding. Can be served with tomato sauce.

MUSHROOM MOUSSAKA

(serves 6)

You can make this hearty mushroom dish, a variation on a Greek and Middle Eastern recipe, with mushrooms from around the world. Try it with wild chantarelle and morel mushrooms (prized in France) — just use reconstituted dry mushrooms if you can't find them fresh. Or how about cooking with mushrooms popular in Asia, like oyster or shiitake? Any mushroom that strikes your fancy will do. Whatever variety you choose, you will end up with a truly multicultural meal!

INGREDIENTS

3 medium aubergines, thinly sliced
5 tbsp extra-virgin olive oil
1 large onion, sliced
1 clove garlic, minced
500 g mushrooms, sliced
6 large tomatoes, chopped
1 tbsp red wine vinegar
1 tbsp fresh thyme, chopped
Sea salt and freshly ground pepper

500 g potatoes, peeled, boiled and sliced
500 g ricotta cheese
6 tbsp mozzarella cheese, shredded

METHOD

Preheat oven to 180°C (350°F). Arrange aubergine on a baking sheet, drizzle with 3 tbsp olive oil, sprinkle with salt and bake for 15 minutes.

Heat remaining oil in a pan and sauté onion and garlic for 10 minutes over medium-low heat, until soft. Add mushrooms and cook until soft, 5 to 10 minutes. Add tomatoes, vinegar, thyme, and salt and pepper to taste, and simmer for 5 minutes.

In a shallow baking dish (preferably 30 × 20 × 3 centimetres), arrange half the potato slices in a thin layer. Add layers of aubergine, mushrooms, and the remaining potatoes. Press down. Top with ricotta cheese and spread evenly, then sprinkle with mozzarella. Bake for 40 to 45 minutes — leave to cool and serve.

MUSHROOM FRITTATA

(serves 8)

This simple egg dish can serve equally well as supper, breakfast or brunch. You can add other vegetables, cheeses or even diced meats of your choosing, based on whatever you have on hand.

INGREDIENTS

Butter or olive oil for pan

60 g spinach leaves, torn into bite-size pieces

120 g mushrooms of your choice (button, portobello and cremini are all great picks), thinly sliced

30 g black olives, sliced

9 large eggs

Salt and pepper, to taste

4 tbsp cheddar cheese, grated

METHOD

Preheat oven to 200°C (400°F). Grease a round baking pan or cast-iron frying pan with butter or oil. Arrange spinach, mushrooms and olives evenly in pan. Whisk eggs and a dash of salt and pepper, pour the eggs over the vegetables, sprinkle with cheese. Bake for 35 minutes or until golden brown and eggs are set in middle. Serve right away.

MUSHROOM QUESADILLA

(serves 4)

A simple, spicy mushroom dish to whip up for lunch or dinner. You can add any ingredients you might enjoy on tacos — like avocado, chilli pepper, sour cream, or fresh coriander — if it strikes your fancy!

INGREDIENTS

1 tbsp extra-virgin olive oil

60 g white mushrooms, sliced

Salt, to taste

4 flour tortillas

4 tbsp salsa

4 tbsp Monterey Jack cheese, grated

4 tbsp black olives, sliced

METHOD

Heat oil in a large saucepan over a medium heat. Sauté mushrooms for 5 minutes until golden, and salt to taste. Lay out tortillas and top one half of each tortilla with mushrooms and one tbsp each salsa, cheese and olives. Fold remaining half of tortilla over onto the filling. Use a spatula to place tortillas in hot pan, cook 2 to 3 minutes, flip and cook an additional minute until cheese is melted and tortilla is golden brown. Eat and enjoy right away.

ROASTED MUSHROOMS AND PEPPERS

(serves 4 as a side)

Served over rocket with a balsamic flavour, this dish bridges the gap between roast vegetables and a salad.

INGREDIENTS

3 large bell peppers, cut into large flat pieces

4 large portobello mushrooms

3 tbsp extra-virgin olive oil

2 tbsp balsamic vinegar

Salt and freshly ground pepper, to taste

120 g rocket leaves

METHOD

Arrange peppers and mushrooms on a foil-lined baking tray, peppers with skins up and mushrooms with caps up. Grill vegetables for 5 minutes, then turn the sheet and grill for another 5 to 7 minutes or until peppers are charred. Remove from heat and let them cool. Peel peppers and discard peel if desired, then slice peppers and mushrooms into thin strips. Combine peppers, mushrooms, olive oil, vinegar, and salt and pepper to taste. Let chill in the refrigerator several hours so vegetables absorb the sweet vinegary flavour. Divide rocket among four plates, top with roasted vegetables and serve.

SAUTÉED MUSHROOMS AND GARLIC

(serves 4 as a side)

Here is the formula for perfect sautéed mushrooms — a classic accompaniment to steak, but also delicious on their own, atop rice or pasta, or with other vegetables.

INGREDIENTS

2 tbsp extra-virgin olive oil

60 g mixed mushrooms, sliced – white button mushrooms, cremini, oyster, chanterelle, or other wild mushrooms will all work

¼ tsp sea salt

1 garlic clove, minced

4 tbsp fresh herb of choice, finely chopped – basil, rosemary, thyme or sage are all great ideas

METHOD

Heat oil in a large sauté pan over a medium heat. Add mushrooms and salt and toss to coat. Cook without stirring 2 to 3 minutes, or until mushrooms begin to brown, then continue to cook while stirring occasionally until soft and golden brown, about 5 to 8 minutes. Reduce heat, add garlic and herbs and cook an additional minute. Serve hot.

SHIITAKE MUSHROOM "BACON"

(serves 4 as a side)

With their rich, savoury, meaty taste and texture, shiitake mushrooms make a perfect bacon substitute when baked until crispy!

INGREDIENTS

120 g shiitake mushrooms, thinly sliced
6 tbsp olive oil
2 tsp soy sauce
Salt and pepper, to taste

METHOD

Preheat oven to 190°C (380°F). Spread mushrooms on baking sheet, drizzle with oil and soy sauce, sprinkle with salt and pepper and toss until coated. Make sure mushrooms are spread out in a single layer and bake 10 to 15 minutes or until shrivelled and crispy, flipping after the first 5 minutes. You can also chop or tear shiitake "bacon" into tiny bits and use like bacon bits on salads, baked potatoes and more!

BROCCOLI AND MUSHROOM STIR-FRY

(serves 4 as a side)

This simple, healthy side dish works particularly well with mushrooms popular in Asian cuisine, such as oyster or shiitake.

INGREDIENTS

2 tbsp sesame oil
1 garlic clove, minced
1 bunch broccoli, separated into florets
200 ml chicken or vegetable stock
60 g assorted mushrooms, sliced
2 tbsp oyster or soy sauce

METHOD

Add sesame oil to wok, warm over high heat, add garlic and stir-fry for 10 seconds. Add broccoli and stir-fry 1 minute. Add a splash of stock and cook, stirring constantly, for 3 minutes, adding the remaining stock gradually whenever it boils away. Add mushrooms and oyster or soy sauce, cover and simmer for 2 minutes. Remove from heat and serve alone or over rice.

MUSHROOM AND POTATO SALAD

(serves 4 to 6 as a side)

This delicious cold salad is a great choice for a summer picnic or potluck!

INGREDIENTS

1 tbsp extra-virgin olive oil

225 g small button mushrooms, halved if larger than bite sized

1 small red bell pepper, chopped

Salt and pepper, to taste

450 g small new potatoes, boiled, halved if larger than bite sized

Honey-mustard dressing, or vinaigrette

METHOD

Heat olive oil in saucepan over medium heat, add mushrooms and cook 7 to 10 minutes or until tender. Add red pepper for 2 to 3 additional minutes, then season with salt and pepper. Combine with boiled potatoes, top with dressing of choice, and chill to let flavours infuse before serving.

CREAMY FRESH MUSHROOM SAUCE

(serves 4 as a side)

This sauce is thick and creamy, perfect with small pasta shapes, rice or vegetables.

INGREDIENTS

2 tbsp extra-virgin olive oil
60 g sliced mushrooms, any varieties
Salt and pepper, to taste
2 tbsp fresh sage, chopped
240 g sour cream or unsweetened, plain Greek yogurt
2 tbsp fresh lemon juice

METHOD

Heat oil in saucepan and sauté mushrooms 3 to 4 minutes — don't let them get too soft. Add salt and pepper to taste, then add sage and stir. Gradually stir in sour cream or yogurt and lemon juice, then remove from heat and serve warm or at room temperature.

PORCINI MUSHROOM PATÉ

(serves 4)

Dried porcini mushrooms make a delicious, richly flavoured vegan paté!

INGREDIENTS

60 g dried porcini mushrooms

2 tbsp extra-virgin olive oil

1 tbsp fresh rosemary, chopped

1 clove garlic, chopped

2 shallots, chopped

30 g raw almonds, chopped

½ tsp salt

METHOD

Soak porcini mushrooms in enough hot water to cover mushrooms, then drain and discard liquid. Heat oil in a small pan, cook rosemary and garlic over low heat for 5 minutes. Meanwhile, place mushrooms and shallots in food processor and grind to a paste. Add cooked rosemary and garlic to food processor and pulse. Return pan to stove, add almonds and toast 2 to 3 minutes. Add nuts and salt to food processor and pulse to combine. Serve with toast or crackers.

JAPANESE-STYLE PICKLED SHIITAKE MUSHROOMS

(serves 12)

These delicious pickled/marinated mushrooms can be eaten alone or added to salads, stir-fries and more.

INGREDIENTS

80 g dried shiitake mushrooms

3 tbsp white or brown sugar (brown sugar gives a richer flavour)

4 tbsp soy sauce

4 tbsp rice vinegar

1 tbsp mirin

2 tsp fresh ginger, chopped

1 tsp toasted black sesame seeds

METHOD

Cover dried mushrooms with 250 ml hot water, soak for 15 minutes, drain and reserve liquid. Combine mushrooms, soaking liquid, sugar, soy sauce, vinegar, mirin and ginger in a saucepan and boil. Reduce heat and simmer for 20 minutes. Remove from heat, drain, but reserve liquid. Slice mushrooms, place in a glass jar, pour cooking liquid over the top and sprinkle with sesame seeds. Leave to cool, then refrigerate for at least 8 hours before enjoying. Lasts two to three weeks when refrigerated.

CREAMY DRIED MUSHROOM SAUCE

(serves 4)

This sauce is made with dried mushrooms, meaning you can choose the most exotic of mushrooms — chanterelles, morels, or even truffles — to get a rich, delicious flavour. Serve this sauce over meat, tofu or pasta.

INGREDIENTS

30 g dried mushrooms, any variety or mixed

2 tbsp extra-virgin olive oil

4 tbsp shallots or chives, chopped

1 clove garlic, minced

375 ml heavy whipping cream, or oat milk for a non-dairy option

Salt and pepper, to taste

METHOD

Soak mushrooms in 125 ml hot water for 20 minutes. Strain, reserving liquid, and chop. Place olive oil in a sauté pan over medium heat, add shallots or chives and cook several minutes until tender. Add garlic and cook additional 1 minute. Add mushrooms and mushroom liquid and cook until liquids are almost evaporated, about 2 minutes. Add cream and simmer 5 minutes or until thickened. Season with salt and pepper to taste.

MUSHROOM "KETCHUP"

(serves 12)

Use dried mushrooms to make this savoury sauce great on burgers, veggie burgers or for dipping French fries. You'll need to grind your dried mushrooms to a powder, which you can do in a food processor or blender.

INGREDIENTS

2 tbsp extra-virgin olive oil
1 large onion, chopped
½ tsp salt
1 clove garlic, chopped
3 tbsp tomato paste

8 g dried porcini
or other mushrooms,
ground to a powder
¼ tsp pepper
32 g nutritional yeast

METHOD

Cook onion and salt in oil over medium high heat, stirring often, until dark golden brown, 15 to 20 minutes. Add garlic and cook for 30 seconds. Stir in 240 ml water, tomato paste, mushroom and pepper, and cook until thick, 15 to 20 minutes. Remove from heat, stir in nutritional yeast, let sit 10 minutes, then blend in food processor or blender until smooth. Keeps refrigerated up to one week.

MUSHROOMS FOR DESSERT

While most fungi would be out of place in a sweet treat, one very special mushroom, the candy cap, tastes and smells almost exactly like maple syrup! Although this mushroom is hard to find fresh, it is available dried online and in speciality grocers, and adds a natural sweetness to desserts. (Of course, as with any dried mushroom, make sure to buy from reputable sources.) You can use a food processor to grind the candy cap into a powder, or buy it already powdered online, and add a small amount to your favourite dessert recipe for a maple flavour. Or use the mushroom whole, as in the candy cap bread pudding recipe below.

CANDY CAP BREAD PUDDING

INGREDIENTS

40 g dried candy cap mushrooms, broken into bite-sized chunks

Butter, to grease the pan

120 g packed brown sugar

2 eggs and 3 additional egg yolks

2 tsp vanilla extract

750 ml whole milk or half and half, or oat milk for a dairy-free option

12 slices cinnamon raisin bread, or bread variety of your choice, cubed

2 tsp cinnamon, plus extra for sprinkling

Whipped cream or vanilla ice cream, to serve

METHOD

Cover mushrooms with hot water and soak for 30 minutes; drain and discard liquid. Meanwhile, preheat oven to 170°C (350°F) and butter a 28 × 18 × 5 cm baking pan.

In a large bowl, whisk together sugar, eggs and vanilla, then gradually add milk or half and half. Add mushrooms, bread cubes and cinnamon and fold together. Let sit 30 minutes so the bread can soak up the liquid, and the candy cap flavour can infuse the other ingredients.

Spread bread-mushroom mixture in baking pan and sprinkle with additional cinnamon. Place pan atop a large roasting pan or baking tray with raised edges, and place in oven. Pour water into roasting pan to a height of 1.5 cm. Bake for 45 to 60 minutes until centre of pudding is firm and top is golden brown. Serve warm with optional whipped cream or vanilla ice cream.

CONCLUSION

With luck, this book has left you with a newfound enthusiasm and curiosity for mushrooms that you can carry with you through everyday life. Perhaps you've been encouraged to look out for mushrooms on your daily walk, try a medicinal mushroom tea or sample wild fungi from a farmer's market in a new recipe. When you see a mushroom, you might now picture the mycelial network descending beneath the earth and linking plants together. You might imagine the possibilities for cleaning up pollution, healing your own body or creating new building materials to use in this world and outer space.

As you continue to explore the world of fungi, remember that mushrooms can only help us if we help them — by showing respect for fungi, and for all organisms and other aspects of the natural world. Due to the actions of humans, the natural world is in peril and mushrooms may offer us a chance to repair some of the damage we've done — but only if we start to take care of these life forms and their environment.

The magic of mushrooms shows us how much nature has left to teach and offer us, how much we have yet to discover and how much we stand to lose if we don't take better care of the world we live in.

Hopefully this book has opened your eyes to the wonders of the fungi kingdom and left you eager to make mushrooms a lasting part of your life.

Have you enjoyed this book?
If so, find us on Facebook at
Summersdale Publishers, on Twitter
at **@Summersdale** and on Instagram at
@summersdalebooks and get in touch.
We'd love to hear from you!

www.summersdale.com

IMAGE CREDITS